THE ROYAL HORTICULTURAL SOCIETY

DIARY 2007

Commentary by
Brent Elliott

Illustrations from
the Royal Horticultural Society's
Lindley Library

F

FRANCES LINCOLN LIMITED
PUBLISHERS

Frances Lincoln Limited
4 Torriano Mews
Torriano Avenue
London NW5 2RZ
www.franceslincoln.com

The Royal Horticultural Society Diary 2007
Copyright © Frances Lincoln Limited 2006

British Library cataloguing-in-publication data
A catalogue record for this book is available from the British Library

ISBN 10: 0-7112-2616-4
ISBN 13: 978-0-7112-2616-6

Printed in China
First Frances Lincoln edition 2006

RHS FLOWER SHOWS 2007

All shows feature a wide range of floral exhibits staged by the nursery trade, with
associated competitions reflecting seasonal changes and horticultural sundries. With the
exception of the shows held at Cardiff, Malvern, Chelsea, Hampton Court, Tatton Park
and Wisley, all RHS Flower Shows will be held in one or both of the Society's
Horticultural Halls in Greycoat Street and Vincent Square, Westminster, London SW1.

**The dates given are correct at the time of going to press, but before travelling to
a show, we strongly advise you to check with the Compass section of the RHS
journal *The Garden*, or telephone the 24-hour Flower Show Information Line
(020 7649 1885) for the latest details.**

FRONT COVER
Tulip 'Bartlett's Thunderbolt', hand-coloured engraving after Edwin Dalton Smith
from Sweet's *Florist's Guide*, published June 1829

BACK COVER
Carnation 'Hill's Duke of Leeds', hand-coloured engraving after Edwin Dalton Smith
from Sweet's *Florist's Guide*, published September 1830

TITLE PAGE
Primula villosa, hand-coloured engraving after Edwin Dalton Smith
from Sweet's *British Flower Garden*, second series, published June 1830

OVERLEAF, LEFT
Tulipa maleolens, hand-coloured engraving after Edwin Dalton Smith
from Sweet's *British Flower Garden*, second series, published August 1832

JANUARY

M	T	W	T	F	S	S
1	2	3	4	5	6	7
8	9	10	11	12	13	14
15	16	17	18	19	20	21
22	23	24	25	26	27	28
29	30	31				

FEBRUARY

M	T	W	T	F	S	S
			1	2	3	4
5	6	7	8	9	10	11
12	13	14	15	16	17	18
19	20	21	22	23	24	25
26	27	28				

MARCH

M	T	W	T	F	S	S
			1	2	3	4
5	6	7	8	9	10	11
12	13	14	15	16	17	18
19	20	21	22	23	24	25
26	27	28	29	30	31	

APRIL

M	T	W	T	F	S	S
						1
2	3	4	5	6	7	8
9	10	11	12	13	14	15
16	17	18	19	20	21	22
23	24	25	26	27	28	29
30						

MAY

M	T	W	T	F	S	S
	1	2	3	4	5	6
7	8	9	10	11	12	13
14	15	16	17	18	19	20
21	22	23	24	25	26	27
28	29	30	31			

JUNE

M	T	W	T	F	S	S
				1	2	3
4	5	6	7	8	9	10
11	12	13	14	15	16	17
18	19	20	21	22	23	24
25	26	27	28	29	30	

JULY

M	T	W	T	F	S	S
						1
2	3	4	5	6	7	8
9	10	11	12	13	14	15
16	17	18	19	20	21	22
23	24	25	26	27	28	29
30	31					

AUGUST

M	T	W	T	F	S	S
		1	2	3	4	5
6	7	8	9	10	11	12
13	14	15	16	17	18	19
20	21	22	23	24	25	26
27	28	29	30	31		

SEPTEMBER

M	T	W	T	F	S	S
					1	2
3	4	5	6	7	8	9
10	11	12	13	14	15	16
17	18	19	20	21	22	23
24	25	26	27	28	29	30

OCTOBER

M	T	W	T	F	S	S
1	2	3	4	5	6	7
8	9	10	11	12	13	14
15	16	17	18	19	20	21
22	23	24	25	26	27	28
29	30	31				

NOVEMBER

M	T	W	T	F	S	S
			1	2	3	4
5	6	7	8	9	10	11
12	13	14	15	16	17	18
19	20	21	22	23	24	25
26	27	28	29	30		

DECEMBER

M	T	W	T	F	S	S
					1	2
3	4	5	6	7	8	9
10	11	12	13	14	15	16
17	18	19	20	21	22	23
24	25	26	27	28	29	30
31						

JANUARY

M	T	W	T	F	S	S
	1	2	3	4	5	6
7	8	9	10	11	12	13
14	15	16	17	18	19	20
21	22	23	24	25	26	27
28	29	30	31			

FEBRUARY

M	T	W	T	F	S	S
				1	2	3
4	5	6	7	8	9	10
11	12	13	14	15	16	17
18	19	20	21	22	23	24
25	26	27	28	29		

MARCH

M	T	W	T	F	S	S
					1	2
3	4	5	6	7	8	9
10	11	12	13	14	15	16
17	18	19	20	21	22	23
24	25	26	27	28	29	30
31						

APRIL

M	T	W	T	F	S	S
	1	2	3	4	5	6
7	8	9	10	11	12	13
14	15	16	17	18	19	20
21	22	23	24	25	26	27
28	29	30				

MAY

M	T	W	T	F	S	S
			1	2	3	4
5	6	7	8	9	10	11
12	13	14	15	16	17	18
19	20	21	22	23	24	25
26	27	28	29	30	31	

JUNE

M	T	W	T	F	S	S
						1
2	3	4	5	6	7	8
9	10	11	12	13	14	15
16	17	18	19	20	21	22
23	24	25	26	27	28	29
30						

JULY

M	T	W	T	F	S	S
	1	2	3	4	5	6
7	8	9	10	11	12	13
14	15	16	17	18	19	20
21	22	23	24	25	26	27
28	29	30	31			

AUGUST

M	T	W	T	F	S	S
				1	2	3
4	5	6	7	8	9	10
11	12	13	14	15	16	17
18	19	20	21	22	23	24
25	26	27	28	29	30	31

SEPTEMBER

M	T	W	T	F	S	S
1	2	3	4	5	6	7
8	9	10	11	12	13	14
15	16	17	18	19	20	21
22	23	24	25	26	27	28
29	30					

OCTOBER

M	T	W	T	F	S	S
		1	2	3	4	5
6	7	8	9	10	11	12
13	14	15	16	17	18	19
20	21	22	23	24	25	26
27	28	29	30	31		

NOVEMBER

M	T	W	T	F	S	S
					1	2
3	4	5	6	7	8	9
10	11	12	13	14	15	16
17	18	19	20	21	22	23
24	25	26	27	28	29	30

DECEMBER

M	T	W	T	F	S	S
1	2	3	4	5	6	7
8	9	10	11	12	13	14
15	16	17	18	19	20	21
22	23	24	25	26	27	28
29	30	31				

Robert Sweet, from whose illustrated works the pictures in this diary are taken, was born in 1782 near Torquay. After working as a gardener at various private estates, he became a partner in William Malcolm's famous nursery at Stockwell and in 1815 became foreman in Reginald Whitley's nursery in Fulham, before finally moving to James Colvill's nursery in Chelsea. He was evidently a skilled cultivator, and Colvill's nursery became famous during his administration for its collection of exotic plants.

Sweet began his literary career in 1818, with a book entitled *Hortus Suburbanus Londinensis; or, a Catalogue of Plants Cultivated in the Neighbourhood of London*. As the name suggests, it was a classified list of plants available in cultivation from the London nurseries in the years after the Napoleonic Wars.

By 1820 it was obvious that there was a market for illustrated works on plants, and Sweet began publication of *Geraniaceae* (1820–30), a part-work issued in monthly instalments. The artist for almost all the 500 coloured plates was Edwin Dalton Smith (1800–post 1866).

In 1823 Sweet embarked on a new venture, *The British Flower Garden: containing Coloured Figures and Descriptions of the most Ornamental and Curious Hardy Herbaceous Plants* (1823–37). Edwin Dalton Smith made many of the plates for this work and he was joined by his brother Frederick W. Smith as well as J. Hart and J. T. Hart (no one knows whether this was a single artist signing his name in two different ways or two different artists). In 1825 Sweet started yet another work, *Cistineae: the Natural Order of Cistus, or Rock-rose* (1825–30).

Disaster struck in 1827, when Sweet was arrested on suspicion of receiving plants stolen from the Royal Botanic Gardens, Kew. Colvill's had come to be a place where people brought plants of potential interest for the nursery to grow on, in the hope that Sweet would write them up, so it is entirely possible that stolen plants could have entered the nursery unknown to the staff; but it has also been suggested that Sweet was deliberately framed. At any rate, he was tried for receiving seven stolen plants and their pots, for a total value of £7 0s. 6d. – an amount that made the crime a capital offence. If he had been found guilty, he could have been hanged. He was acquitted, and the published account of his trial shows that one juror asked pointed questions about whether Sweet had criticized William Townsend Aiton, the director of Kew.

After the trial, Sweet left Colvill's, and thereafter had to rely on his pen as his source of income. In 1827 he started two more publications: *Flora Australasica* (1827–8) and *The Florist's Guide* (1827–31), a work devoted to 'florists' flowers' such as tulips, auriculas and ranunculus. In 1830 his mental health gave way and he died at Chelsea on 22 January 1835. His name lives on in the name of the tropical tree genus *Sweetia*, and in his many publications, which are still sought after for their illustrations and as a record of early nineteenth-century horticulture.

Brent Elliott
The Royal Horticultural Society

JANUARY

1 MONDAY

New Year's Day
Holiday, UK, Republic of Ireland, Canada,
USA, Australia and New Zealand

2 TUESDAY

Holiday, Scotland and New Zealand

3 WEDNESDAY

Full Moon

4 THURSDAY

5 FRIDAY

6 SATURDAY

Epiphany

7 SUNDAY

Helleborus purpurascens, hand-coloured engraving after Edwin Dalton Smith
from Sweet's *British Flower Garden*, second series, published May 1832

JANUARY

8 MONDAY

9 TUESDAY

10 WEDNESDAY

11 THURSDAY

Last Quarter

12 FRIDAY

13 SATURDAY

14 SUNDAY

Hyacinth 'Porcelaine Sceptre', hand-coloured engraving after Edwin Dalton Smith
from Sweet's *Florist's Guide*, published July 1828

15 MONDAY

Holiday, USA (Martin Luther King's birthday)

16 TUESDAY

RHS London Flower Show

17 WEDNESDAY

RHS London Flower Show

18 THURSDAY

19 FRIDAY

New Moon

20 SATURDAY

Islamic New Year (subject to sighting of the moon)

21 SUNDAY

Habranthus robustus (now *Hippeastrum robustum*), hand-coloured engraving after William Herbert
from Sweet's *British Flower Garden*, second series, published September 1829

JANUARY

22 MONDAY

23 TUESDAY

24 WEDNESDAY

25 THURSDAY

First Quarter

26 FRIDAY

Holiday, Australia (Australia Day)

27 SATURDAY

28 SUNDAY

Crocus suaveolens, hand-coloured engraving after J. T. Hart
from Sweet's *British Flower Garden*, second series, published September 1836

JANUARY & FEBRUARY

29 MONDAY

30 TUESDAY

31 WEDNESDAY

1 THURSDAY

2 FRIDAY

Full Moon

3 SATURDAY

4 SUNDAY

Hyacinth 'Yellow Ophir', hand-coloured engraving after Edwin Dalton Smith
from Sweet's *Florist's Guide*, published January 1830

FEBRUARY

5 MONDAY

6 TUESDAY

Holiday, New Zealand (Waitangi Day)

7 WEDNESDAY

8 THURSDAY

9 FRIDAY

10 SATURDAY

Last Quarter

11 SUNDAY

Daphne odora var. *rubra,* hand-coloured engraving after J. Hart
from Sweet's *British Flower Garden*, second series, published January 1836

FEBRUARY

12 MONDAY

Holiday, USA (Lincoln's birthday)

13 TUESDAY

RHS London Flower Show

14 WEDNESDAY

St Valentine's Day
RHS London Flower Show

15 THURSDAY

16 FRIDAY

17 SATURDAY

New Moon

18 SUNDAY

Chinese New Year

Polyanthus 'Fletcher's Defiance', hand-coloured engraving after Edwin Dalton Smith
from Sweet's *Florist's Guide*, published July 1828

FEBRUARY

---

19 MONDAY

Holiday, USA (Presidents' Day)

---

20 TUESDAY

Shrove Tuesday

---

21 WEDNESDAY

Ash Wednesday

---

22 THURSDAY

---

23 FRIDAY

---

24 SATURDAY

First Quarter

---

25 SUNDAY

Camellia japonica var. *sweetiana,* hand-coloured engraving after Edwin Dalton Smith
from Sweet's *British Flower Garden,* second series, published March 1832

FEBRUARY & MARCH

26 MONDAY

27 TUESDAY

28 WEDNESDAY

1 THURSDAY

St David's Day

2 FRIDAY

3 SATURDAY

Full Moon

4 SUNDAY

Rhododendron sinense var. *flavescens*, hand-coloured engraving after Edwin Dalton Smith
from Sweet's *British Flower Garden*, published March 1829

MARCH

5 MONDAY

6 TUESDAY

7 WEDNESDAY

8 THURSDAY

9 FRIDAY

10 SATURDAY

11 SUNDAY

Anemone stellata (now *Anemone hortensis*), hand-coloured engraving after Edwin Dalton Smith from Sweet's *British Flower Garden*, published June 1825

MARCH

12 MONDAY

Commonwealth Day
Last Quarter

13 TUESDAY

RHS London Flower Show

14 WEDNESDAY

RHS London Flower Show

15 THURSDAY

16 FRIDAY

17 SATURDAY

RHS London Orchid Show

18 SUNDAY

Mothering Sunday, UK
RHS London Orchid Show

Ajax pumilus (now *Narcissus pseudonarcissus*), hand-coloured engraving after Edwin Dalton Sm
from Sweet's *British Flower Garden*, second series, published May 1

MARCH

19 MONDAY

St Patrick's Day
Holiday, Northern Ireland and Republic of Ireland
New Moon

20 TUESDAY

21 WEDNESDAY

Vernal Equinox

22 THURSDAY

23 FRIDAY

24 SATURDAY

25 SUNDAY

British Summertime begins
First Quarter

Rhododendron arboreum, hand-coloured engraving after Edwin Dalton Smith
from Sweet's *British Flower Garden*, published May 1828

MARCH & APRIL

26 MONDAY

27 TUESDAY

28 WEDNESDAY

29 THURSDAY

30 FRIDAY

31 SATURDAY

1 SUNDAY

Palm Sunday

Viola cucullata, hand-coloured engraving after J. Hart
from Sweet's *British Flower Garden*, second series, published August 1835

APRIL

2 MONDAY

Full Moon

3 TUESDAY

Passover (Pesach), First Day
RHS London Flower Show

4 WEDNESDAY

RHS London Flower Show

5 THURSDAY

Maundy Thursday

6 FRIDAY

Good Friday
Holiday, UK, Republic of Ireland, Canada, USA,
Australia and New Zealand

7 SATURDAY

8 SUNDAY

Easter Sunday

Auricula 'Howe's Venus', hand-coloured engraving after Edwin Dalton Smith
from Sweet's *Florist's Guide*, published March 1829

APRIL

9 MONDAY

Easter Monday
Holiday, UK (exc. Scotland), Republic of Ireland,
Canada, Australia and New Zealand
Passover (Pesach), Seventh Day

10 TUESDAY

Passover (Pesach), Eighth Day
Last Quarter

11 WEDNESDAY

12 THURSDAY

13 FRIDAY

14 SATURDAY

15 SUNDAY

Magnolia × soulangeana, hand-coloured engraving after Edwin Dalton Smith
from Sweet's *British Flower Garden*, published July 1828

APRIL

16 MONDAY

17 TUESDAY

New Moon

18 WEDNESDAY

19 THURSDAY

20 FRIDAY

RHS Spring Flower Show, Cardiff (to be confirmed)

21 SATURDAY

Birthday of Queen Elizabeth II
RHS Spring Flower Show, Cardiff (to be confirmed)

22 SUNDAY

RHS Spring Flower Show, Cardiff (to be confirmed)

Tulip 'Alexandrina', hand-coloured engraving after Edwin Dalton Smith
from Sweet's *Florist's Guide*, published May 1830

APRIL

---

23 MONDAY

St George's Day

---

24 TUESDAY

RHS Late Daffodil Competition, Wisley
First Quarter

---

25 WEDNESDAY

Holiday, Australia and New Zealand (Anzac Day)
RHS Late Daffodil Competition, Wisley

---

26 THURSDAY

---

27 FRIDAY

---

28 SATURDAY

---

29 SUNDAY

Orchis militaris, hand-coloured engraving after Edwin Dalton Smith
from Sweet's *British Flower Garden*, published July 1826

APRIL & MAY

30 MONDAY

1 TUESDAY

2 WEDNESDAY

Full Moon

3 THURSDAY

4 FRIDAY

5 SAT JRDAY

6 SU JDAY

tian', hand-coloured engraving after Edwin Dalton Smith
veet's *Florist's Guide*, published October 1829

MAY

7 MONDAY

Early May Bank Holiday, UK and Republic of Ireland

8 TUESDAY

9 WEDNESDAY

10 THURSDAY

Malvern Spring Gardening Show
Last Quarter

11 FRIDAY

Malvern Spring Gardening Show

12 SATURDAY

Malvern Spring Gardening Show

13 SUNDAY

Mother's Day, Canada, USA, Australia and New Zealand
Malvern Spring Gardening Show

Wisteria chinensis, hand-coloured engraving after Edwin Dalton Smith
from Sweet's *British Flower Garden,* published July 1827

MAY

14 MONDAY

15 TUESDAY

16 WEDNESDAY

New Moon

17 THURSDAY

Ascension Day

18 FRIDAY

19 SATURDAY

20 SUNDAY

Ranunculus 'Maculata Suprema', hand-coloured engraving after Edwin Dalton Smith
from Sweet's *Florist's Guide*, published December 1830

21 MONDAY

22 TUESDAY

Chelsea Flower Show

23 WEDNESDAY

Jewish Feast of Weeks (Shavuot)
Chelsea Flower Show
First Quarter

24 THURSDAY

Chelsea Flower Show

25 FRIDAY

Chelsea Flower Show

26 SATURDAY

Chelsea Flower Show

27 SUNDAY

Whit Sunday (Pentecost)

Iris biflora, hand-coloured engraving after Edwin Dalton Smith
from Sweet's *British Flower Garden*, second series, published July 1832

MAY & JUNE

28 MONDAY

Spring Bank Holiday, UK
Holiday, USA (Memorial Day)

29 TUESDAY

30 WEDNESDAY

31 THURSDAY

1 FRIDAY

Full Moon

2 SATURDAY

3 SUNDAY

Trinity Sunday

Adenophora intermedia (now *Adenophora communis*), hand-coloured engraving after Edwin Dalton Smith from Sweet's *British Flower Garden*, second series, published August 1831

2007

JUNE

---

4 MONDAY

Holiday, Republic of Ireland
Holiday, New Zealand (The Queen's birthday)

---

5 TUESDAY

---

6 WEDNESDAY

---

7 THURSDAY

Corpus Christi

---

8 FRIDAY

Last Quarter

---

9 SATURDAY

The Queen's official birthday (subject to confirmation)

---

10 SUNDAY

JUNE

11 MONDAY

Holiday, Australia (The Queen's birthday)

12 TUESDAY

13 WEDNESDAY

BBC Gardeners' World Live, Birmingham

14 THURSDAY

BBC Gardeners' World Live, Birmingham

15 FRIDAY

BBC Gardeners' World Live, Birmingham
New Moon

16 SATURDAY

BBC Gardeners' World Live, Birmingham

17 SUNDAY

Father's Day, UK, Canada and USA
BBC Gardeners' World Live, Birmingham

Ranunculus 'Julius', hand-coloured engraving after Edwin Dalton Smith
from Sweet's *Florist's Guide*, published November 1828

2007

JUNE

---

18 MONDAY

---

19 TUESDAY

---

20 WEDNESDAY

---

21 THURSDAY

Summer Solstice

22 FRIDAY

First Quarter

23 SATURDAY

---

24 SUNDAY

Aquilegia glandulosa, hand-coloured engraving after Edwin Dalton Smith
from Sweet's *British Flower Garden*, second series, published July 1830

JUNE & JULY

25 MONDAY

26 TUESDAY

27 WEDNESDAY

28 THURSDAY

29 FRIDAY

30 SATURDAY

Full Moon

1 SUNDAY

Pink 'Davey's Juliet', hand-coloured engraving after Edwin Dalton Smith
from Sweet's *Florist's Guide*, published August 1827

2007

JULY

2 MONDAY

Holiday, Canada (Canada Day)

3 TUESDAY

Hampton Court Palace Flower Show

4 WEDNESDAY

Holiday, USA (Independence Day)
Hampton Court Palace Flower Show

5 THURSDAY

Hampton Court Palace Flower Show

6 FRIDAY

Hampton Court Palace Flower Show

7 SATURDAY

Hampton Court Palace Flower Show
Last Quarter

8 SUNDAY

Hampton Court Palace Flower Show

Paeonia tenuifolia var. *plena,* unsigned hand-coloured engraving
from Sweet's *British Flower Garden*, second series, published August 1836

JULY

9 MONDAY

---

10 TUESDAY

---

11 WEDNESDAY

---

12 THURSDAY

Holiday, Northern Ireland (Battle of the Boyne)

---

13 FRIDAY

---

14 SATURDAY

New Moon

---

15 SUNDAY

St Swithin's Day

Eschscholzia crocea (now *Eschscholzia californica*), hand-coloured engraving after J. Hart
from Sweet's *British Flower Garden*, second series, published August 1835

JULY

16 MONDAY

17 TUESDAY

18 WEDNESDAY

The RHS Flower Show at Tatton Park

19 THURSDAY

The RHS Flower Show at Tatton Park

20 FRIDAY

The RHS Flower Show at Tatton Park

21 SATURDAY

The RHS Flower Show at Tatton Park

22 SUNDAY

The RHS Flower Show at Tatton Park
First Quarter

Delphinium cheilantum var. *multiplex*, hand-coloured engraving after J. Hart
from Sweet's *British Flower Garden*, second series, published November 1835

JULY

23 MONDAY

24 TUESDAY

25 WEDNESDAY

26 THURSDAY

27 FRIDAY

28 SATURDAY

29 SUNDAY

Carnation 'Pearson's Rising Sun', hand-coloured engraving after Edwin Dalton Smith
from Sweet's *Florist's Guide*, published June 1829

JULY & AUGUST

30 MONDAY

Full Moon

31 TUESDAY

1 WEDNESDAY

2 THURSDAY

3 FRIDAY

4 SATURDAY

5 SUNDAY

Last Quarter

Platycodon grandiflorum, hand-coloured engraving after J. T. Hart
from Sweet's *British Flower Garden*, second series, published September 1833

AUGUST

---

6 MONDAY

Summer Bank Holiday, Scotland and Republic of Ireland

---

7 TUESDAY

---

8 WEDNESDAY

---

9 THURSDAY

---

10 FRIDAY

---

11 SATURDAY

---

12 SUNDAY

New Moon

Lupinus pulchellus, hand-coloured engraving after Edwin Dalton Smith
from Sweet's *British Flower Garden,* second series, published October 1830

AUGUST

13 MONDAY

14 TUESDAY

15 WEDNESDAY

16 THURSDAY

17 FRIDAY

18 SATURDAY

19 SUNDAY

Phlox corymbosa (now *Phlox paniculata*), hand-coloured engraving after Edwin Dalton Smith
from Sweet's *British Flower Garden*, second series, published October 1831

AUGUST

---

20 MONDAY

First Quarter

---

21 TUESDAY

Wisley Flower Show

---

22 WEDNESDAY

Wisley Flower Show

---

23 THURSDAY

Wisley Flower Show

---

24 FRIDAY

---

25 SATURDAY

---

26 SUNDAY

Clematis florida var. *sieboldii*, hand-coloured engraving after J. T. Hart
from Sweet's *British Flower Garden*, second series, published August 1837

AUGUST & SEPTEMBER

---

27 MONDAY

Summer Bank Holiday, UK (exc. Scotland)

---

28 TUESDAY

Full Moon

---

29 WEDNESDAY

---

30 THURSDAY

---

31 FRIDAY

---

1 SATURDAY

---

2 SUNDAY

Father's Day, Australia and New Zealand

Malope trifida, hand-coloured engraving after Edwin Dalton Smith
from Sweet's *British Flower Garden*, published May 1826

3

SEPTEMBER

---

3 MONDAY

Holiday, Canada (Labour Day) and USA (Labor Day)

---

4 TUESDAY

Last Quarter

---

5 WEDNESDAY

---

6 THURSDAY

---

7 FRIDAY

---

8 SATURDAY

---

9 SUNDAY

Rudbeckia pinnata (now *Ratibida pinnata*), hand-coloured engraving after Edwin Dalton Smith
from Sweet's *British Flower Garden*, published March 1826

2007

SEPTEMBER

---

10 MONDAY

---

11 TUESDAY

RHS London Late Summer Show
New Moon

---

12 WEDNESDAY

RHS London Late Summer Show

---

13 THURSDAY

Jewish New Year (Rosh Hashanah)
First Day of Ramadân (subject to sighting of the moon)

---

14 FRIDAY

---

15 SATURDAY

---

16 SUNDAY

Tropaeolum majus var. *atrosanguineum*, hand-coloured engraving after J. Hart
from Sweet's *British Flower Garden*, second series, published August 1833

SEPTEMBER

17 MONDAY

18 TUESDAY

19 WEDNESDAY

First Quarter

20 THURSDAY

21 FRIDAY

22 SATURDAY

Jewish Day of Atonement (Yom Kippur)

23 SUNDAY

Autumnal Equinox

Tagetes corymbosa (now *Tagetes patula*), hand-coloured engraving after Edwin Dalton Smith
from Sweet's *British Flower Garden*, published April 1826

SEPTEMBER

---

24 MONDAY

---

25 TUESDAY

---

26 WEDNESDAY

Full Moon

---

27 THURSDAY

Jewish Festival of Tabernacles (Succoth), First Day

---

28 FRIDAY

---

29 SATURDAY

Michaelmas Day
Malvern Autumn Show

---

30 SUNDAY

Malvern Autumn Show

Dahlia 'Morning Star', hand-coloured engraving after Edwin Dalton Smith
from Sweet's *Florist's Guide*, published November 1828

OCTOBER

---

1 MONDAY

---

2 TUESDAY

---

3 WEDNESDAY

Last Quarter

---

4 THURSDAY

Jewish Festival of Tabernacles (Succoth), Eighth Day

---

5 FRIDAY

---

6 SATURDAY

---

7 SUNDAY

Gladiolus viperatus (now *Gladiolus orchidiflorus*), hand-coloured engraving after Edwin Dalton Smith
from Sweet's *British Flower Garden*, published May 1826

OCTOBER

8 MONDAY

Holiday, Canada (Thanksgiving Day)
Holiday, USA (Columbus Day)

9 TUESDAY

RHS Great Autumn Show

10 WEDNESDAY

RHS Great Autumn Show

11 THURSDAY

New Moon

12 FRIDAY

13 SATURDAY

14 SUNDAY

Gaillardia picta, hand-coloured engraving after S. Humble
from Sweet's *British Flower Garden*, second series, published December 1834

OCTOBER

15 MONDAY

16 TUESDAY

17 WEDNESDAY

18 THURSDAY

19 FRIDAY

First Quarter

20 SATURDAY

21 SUNDAY

Lubinia atropurpurea (now *Lysimachia nutans*), hand-coloured engraving after Edwin Dalton Smith
from Sweet's *British Flower Garden*, second series, published February 1830

22 MONDAY

Holiday, New Zealand (Labour Day)

23 TUESDAY

24 WEDNESDAY

United Nations Day

25 THURSDAY

26 FRIDAY

Full Moon

27 SATURDAY

28 SUNDAY

British Summertime ends

Verbena chamaedryfolia, hand-coloured engraving after Edwin Dalton Smith
from Sweet's *British Flower Garden,* second series, published August 1829

OCTOBER & NOVEMBER

29 MONDAY

Holiday, Republic of Ireland

30 TUESDAY

31 WEDNESDAY

Hallowe'en

1 THURSDAY

All Saints' Day
Last Quarter

2 FRIDAY

3 SATURDAY

4 SUNDAY

Passiflora colvillii, hand-coloured engraving after Edwin Dalton Smith
from Sweet's *British Flower Garden*, published October 1825

2007

NOVEMBER

5 MONDAY

Guy Fawkes' Day

6 TUESDAY

7 WEDNESDAY

8 THURSDAY

9 FRIDAY

RHS London Flower Show
New Moon

10 SATURDAY

RHS London Flower Show

11 SUNDAY

Remembrance Sunday, UK
Holiday, Canada (Remembrance Day)
and USA (Veterans' Day)

Chrysanthemum sinense var. *fasciculatum,* hand-coloured engraving after Edwin Dalton Smith
from Sweet's *British Flower Garden*, published June 1823

NOVEMBER

12 MONDAY

---

13 TUESDAY

---

14 WEDNESDAY

---

15 THURSDAY

---

16 FRIDAY

---

17 SATURDAY

First Quarter

---

18 SUNDAY

Leptostelma maxima (now *Erigeron maximum*), hand-coloured engraving after Edwin Dalton Smith from Sweet's *British Flower Garden*, second series, published March 1830

19 MONDAY

20 TUESDAY

21 WEDNESDAY

22 THURSDAY

Holiday, USA (Thanksgiving Day)

23 FRIDAY

24 SATURDAY

Full Moon

25 SUNDAY

Cyclamen europaeum, hand-coloured engraving after Edwin Dalton Smith
from Sweet's *British Flower Garden*, published October 1826

NOVEMBER & DECEMBER

26 MONDAY

27 TUESDAY

28 WEDNESDAY

29 THURSDAY

30 FRIDAY

St Andrew's Day

1 SATURDAY

Last Quarter

2 SUNDAY

Advent Sunday

Berberis nervosa, hand-coloured engraving after Edwin Dalton Smith
from Sweet's *British Flower Garden*, second series, published December 1832

DECEMBER

3 MONDAY

4 TUESDAY

5 WEDNESDAY

Jewish Festival of Chanukah, First Day

6 THURSDAY

7 FRIDAY

8 SATURDAY

9 SUNDAY

New Moon

Sarracenia minor (now *Sarracenia sweetii*), hand-coloured engraving after Edwin Dalton Smith
from Sweet's *British Flower Garden*, second series, published April 1832

DECEMBER

10 MONDAY

11 TUESDAY

12 WEDNESDAY

13 THURSDAY

14 FRIDAY

15 SATURDAY

16 SUNDAY

Hermione tereticaulis (now *Narcissus tazetta*), hand-coloured engraving after Edwin Dalton Smith
from Sweet's *British Flower Garden*, second series, published February 1833

17 MONDAY

First Quarter

18 TUESDAY

19 WEDNESDAY

20 THURSDAY

21 FRIDAY

22 SATURDAY

Winter Solstice

23 SUNDAY

Alstroemeria psittacina (now *Alstroemeria pulchella*), hand-coloured engraving after Edwin Dalton Smith
from Sweet's *British Flower Garden*, second series, published September 1829

DECEMBER

24 MONDAY

Christmas Eve
Full Moon

25 TUESDAY

Christmas Day
Holiday, UK, Republic of Ireland, Canada, USA,
Australia and New Zealand

26 WEDNESDAY

Boxing Day (St Stephen's Day)
Holiday, UK, Republic of Ireland, Canada,
Australia and New Zealand

27 THURSDAY

28 FRIDAY

29 SATURDAY

30 SUNDAY

Habranthus roseus (now *Hippeastrum roseum*), hand-coloured engraving after Edwin Dalton Smith
from Sweet's *British Flower Garden*, second series, published August 1831

DECEMBER & JANUARY

31 MONDAY

New Year's Eve
Last Quarter

1 TUESDAY

New Year's Day
Holiday, UK, Republic of Ireland, Canada, USA,
Australia and New Zealand

2 WEDNESDAY

Holiday, Scotland and New Zealand

3 THURSDAY

4 FRIDAY

5 SATURDAY

6 SUNDAY

Epiphany

Brugmansia sanguinea, hand-coloured engraving after J. Hart
from Sweet's *British Flower Garden,* second series, published January 1835

AUSTRIA	JAN. 1, 6; APRIL 8, 9; MAY 1, 28; JUNE 7; AUG. 15; OCT. 26; NOV. 1; DEC. 8, 25, 26
BELGIUM	JAN. 1; APRIL 8, 9; MAY 1, 17, 27, 28; JULY 21; AUG. 15; NOV. 1, 11, 15; DEC. 25, 26
BULGARIA	JAN. 1; MARCH 3; APRIL 9, 21, 23, 24; MAY 1, 6, 24; SEPT. 6, 22; NOV. 1; DEC. 24, 25, 26, 31
CYPRUS	JAN. 1, 6; FEB. 19; MARCH 25; APRIL 1, 6, 8, 9; MAY 1, 27, 28; AUG. 15; OCT. 1, 28; DEC. 25, 26
CZECH REPUBLIC	JAN. 1; APRIL 8, 9; MAY 1, 8; JULY 5, 6; SEPT. 28; OCT. 28; NOV. 17; DEC. 24, 25, 26
DENMARK	JAN. 1; APRIL 5, 6, 8, 9; MAY 4, 17, 27, 28; JUNE 5; DEC. 25, 26
ESTONIA	JAN. 1; FEB. 24; APRIL 6, 8; MAY 1, 27; JUNE 23, 24; AUG. 20; DEC. 24, 25, 26
FINLAND	JAN. 1, 6; APRIL 6, 8, 9; MAY 1, 17, 27; JUNE 23; NOV. 3; DEC. 6, 25, 26
FRANCE	JAN. 1; APRIL 8, 9; MAY 1, 8, 17, 27, 28; JULY 14; AUG. 15; NOV. 1, 11; DEC. 25
GERMANY	JAN. 1; APRIL 6, 8, 9; MAY 1, 17, 27, 28; OCT. 3; DEC. 25, 26
GREECE	JAN. 1, 6; FEB. 19; MARCH 25; APRIL 6, 8, 9; MAY 1, 27, 28; AUG. 15; OCT. 28; DEC. 25, 26
HUNGARY	JAN. 1; MARCH 15; APRIL 8, 9; MAY 1, 27, 28; AUG. 20; OCT. 23; NOV. 1; DEC. 25, 26
ITALY	JAN. 1, 6; APRIL 8, 9, 25; MAY 1; JUNE 2; AUG. 15; NOV. 1; DEC. 8, 25, 26
LATVIA	JAN. 1; APRIL 6, 8, 9; MAY 1, 4; JUNE 23, 24; NOV. 18; DEC. 25, 26, 31
LITHUANIA	JAN. 1; FEB. 16; MARCH 11; APRIL 8, 9; MAY 1; JUNE 24; JULY 6; AUG. 15; NOV. 1; DEC. 25, 26
LUXEMBOURG	JAN. 1; FEB. 19; APRIL 8, 9; MAY 1, 17, 27, 28; JUNE 23; AUG. 15; NOV. 1; DEC. 25, 26
MALTA	JAN. 1; FEB. 10; MARCH 19, 31; APRIL 6, 8; MAY 1; JUNE 7, 29; AUG. 15; SEPT. 8, 21; DEC. 8, 13, 25
NETHERLANDS	JAN. 1; APRIL 6, 8, 9, 30; MAY 5, 17, 27, 28; DEC. 25, 26
NORWAY	JAN. 1; APRIL 5, 6, 8, 9; MAY 1, 17, 27, 28; DEC. 25, 26
POLAND	JAN. 1; APRIL 8, 9; MAY 1, 3; JUNE 7; AUG. 15; NOV. 1, 11; DEC. 25, 26
PORTUGAL	JAN. 1; FEB. 20; APRIL 6, 8, 9, 25; MAY 1; JUNE 7, 10; AUG. 15; OCT. 5; NOV. 1; DEC. 1, 8, 25
ROMANIA	JAN. 1,2; APRIL 9, 23, 24; MAY 1; DEC. 1, 25, 26
SLOVAKIA	JAN. 1, 6; APRIL 6, 8, 9; MAY 1, 8; JULY 5; AUG. 29; SEPT. 1, 15; NOV. 1, 17; DEC. 24, 25, 26
SLOVENIA	JAN. 1, 2; FEB. 8; APRIL 8, 9, 27; MAY 1, 2, 27; JUNE 27; AUG. 15; OCT. 31; NOV. 1; DEC. 25, 26
SPAIN	JAN. 1, 6; MAY 19; APRIL 6, 8; MAY 1, 27; AUG. 15; OCT. 12; NOV. 1; DEC. 6, 8, 25
SWEDEN	JAN. 1, 6; APRIL 6, 8, 9; MAY 1, 17, 27; JUNE 6, 23; NOV. 3; DEC. 25, 26
SWITZERLAND	JAN. 1; APRIL 6, 8, 9; MAY 1, 17, 27, 28; AUG. 1; DEC. 25, 26